D1529246

Reptiles and Amphibians

Text: Sharon Dalgleish

Consultant: George McKay, Conservation Biologist

This edition first published 2003 by

MASON CREST PUBLISHERS INC.

370 Reed Road

Broomall, PA 19008

All rights reserved. No part of this publication may be reproduced
or transmitted in any form or by any means, electronic or mechanical,
including photocopying, recording, taping, or any information storage and
retrieval system, without permission in writing from the publisher.

© Weldon Owen Inc.

Conceived and produced by

Weldon Owen Pty Limited

Library of Congress Cataloging-in-Publication Data

on file at the Library of Congress

ISBN: 1-59084-196-4

Printed in Singapore.

1 2 3 4 5 6 7 8 9 06 05 04 03

CONTENTS

FISHY BEGINNINGS

Frogs and newts belong to a class of animals called amphibians—animals that live part of their life on land and part in the water. Amphibians evolved from fish about 360 million years ago. They crawled out of the sea and onto the land. They had lungs and strong fins, but they still had to lay their jellylike eggs in water. About 300 million years ago, some of these amphibians began producing eggs that could be laid on land. These amphibians became the first reptiles.

trilobites

Pteraspis

Drepanaspis

scorpion

DID YOU KNOW?

Eusthenopteron was a fish that had lungs as well as gills. It also had bones and muscles in its fins. These were the first legs! It could move on land and breathe air.

THE ROAD TO REPTILES

Fish had to change a lot before they could
leave their watery home for a home on dry land.
Once they were able to live on land, reptiles
dominated the world for millions of years.

Dunkleosteus

Dimetrodon

Ichthyostega

dragonfly

Hylonomus

Ornithosuchus

THE AGE OF DINOSAURS

Dinosaurs were reptiles. Some were as small as a chicken, while others were as tall as a four-story building. Like other reptiles, dinosaurs had scaly skins and laid their eggs in shells. Some dinosaurs walked on four legs, and some could walk on two legs. Unlike other reptiles, whose legs sprawl out sideways, dinosaurs walked with their legs upright beneath their bodies. Dinosaurs could travel further and faster than any other reptile.

TWO LEGS OR FOUR?

Euparkeria had straight legs and carried its body off the ground. Lagosuchus could walk on its hind legs. Eoraptor was the earliest known dinosaur.

Euparkeria   Lagosuchus   Eoraptor

Sprawling
Dinosaurs developed from animals that sprawled on four legs.

Half and Half
Some reptiles, such as crocodiles, have upright back legs and sprawling front legs.

On Two Legs
A dinosaur's weight was balanced over the hips by its tail.

IN THE AIR

Pterosaurs flew on wings made of skin. They were the first animals with backbones to fly. The earliest bird with feathers, Archaeopteryx, was related to the dinosaurs.

Pteranodon

Dimorphodon

Archaeopteryx

Rhamphorhynchus

At the same time that dinosaurs ruled the land, marine reptiles were swimming in the sea, and flying reptiles called pterosaurs were gliding through the air. Many pterosaurs hunted fish. Pteranodon probably scooped up fish just like a modern pelican. Some marine reptiles ate smaller sea creatures, while others ate larger prey. Some marine reptiles are distant cousins of dinosaurs.

IN THE SEA

The turtle Archelon was as big as a car. Deinosuchus was a giant crocodile, about 50 feet (15 meters) long. Other marine reptiles looked like dinosaurs with fins.

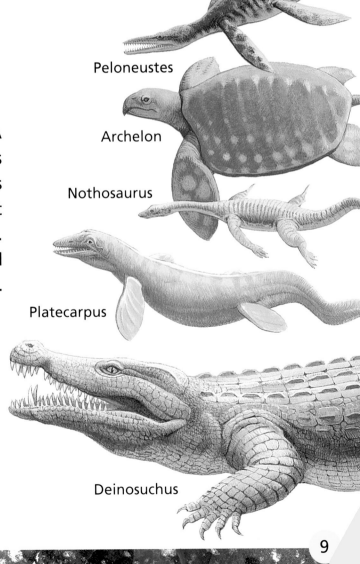

Peloneustes

Archelon

Nothosaurus

Platecarpus

Deinosuchus

CREEPING CRAWLIES

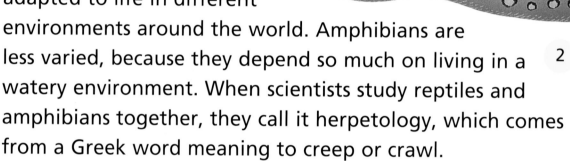

Modern reptiles come in a huge variety of sizes and shapes, and have adapted to life in different environments around the world. Amphibians are less varied, because they depend so much on living in a watery environment. When scientists study reptiles and amphibians together, they call it herpetology, which comes from a Greek word meaning to creep or crawl.

1

2

INSIDE AN EGG

Amphibian and reptile eggs both have a yolk to feed the growing young. A reptile egg has a tough shell, but an amphibian egg has only jelly to protect it.

REPTILE EGG

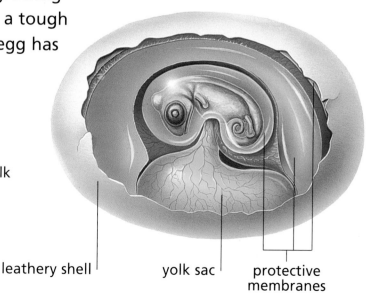

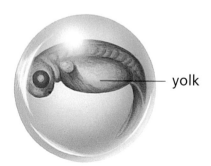

yolk

AMPHIBIAN EGG

leathery shell

yolk sac

protective membranes

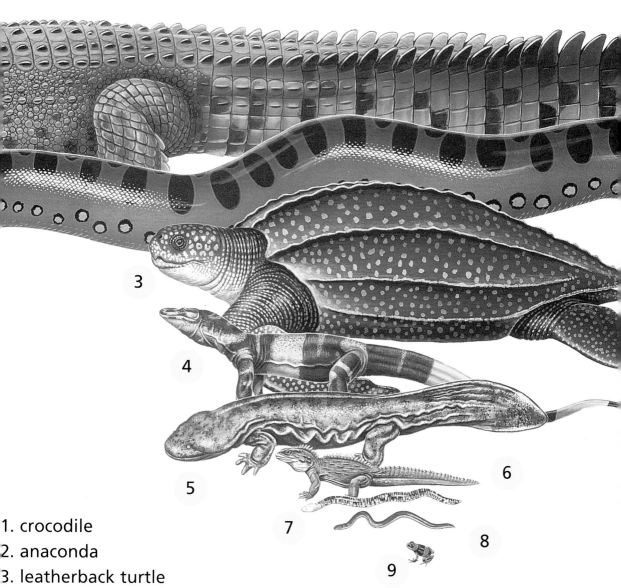

1. crocodile
2. anaconda
3. leatherback turtle
4. monitor lizard
5. salamander
6. tuatara
7. worm lizard
8. caecilian
9. poison-dart frog

Lizards stay warm on cloudy afternoons by pressing against rocks that have soaked up heat from earlier in the day.

COLD NIGHTS

A cold-blooded reptile must lie in the sun before it is warm enough to move quickly. A warm-blooded mammal can be active all the time.

TEMPERATURE CONTROL

Reptiles are cold-blooded animals. To warm up, they have to move into the sun or onto a warm surface. To cool down, they move into the shade. Reptiles use a lot of energy only when they are warm and active. In very cold weather, their heart rate slows down, they breathe slowly, and they even stop digesting food to save energy.

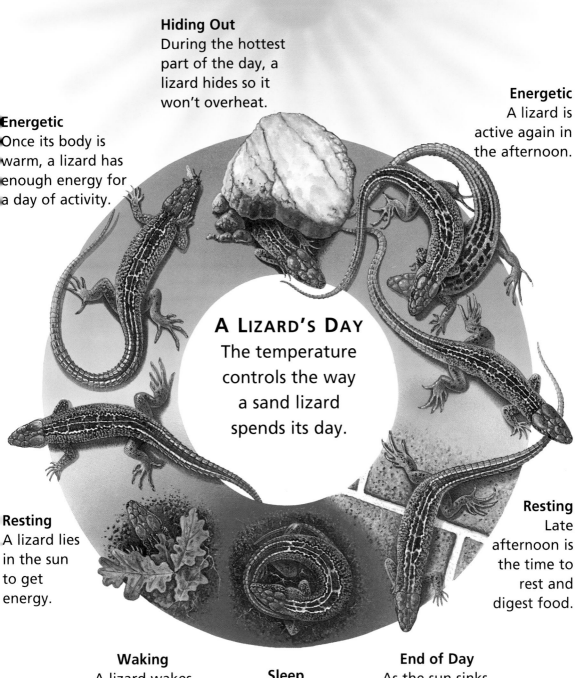

Hiding Out
During the hottest part of the day, a lizard hides so it won't overheat.

Energetic
A lizard is active again in the afternoon.

Energetic
Once its body is warm, a lizard has enough energy for a day of activity.

A LIZARD'S DAY
The temperature controls the way a sand lizard spends its day.

Resting
A lizard lies in the sun to get energy.

Resting
Late afternoon is the time to rest and digest food.

Waking
A lizard wakes with the sun.

Sleep
During the night, a lizard curls up for protection.

End of Day
As the sun sinks, a lizard heads for its shelter.

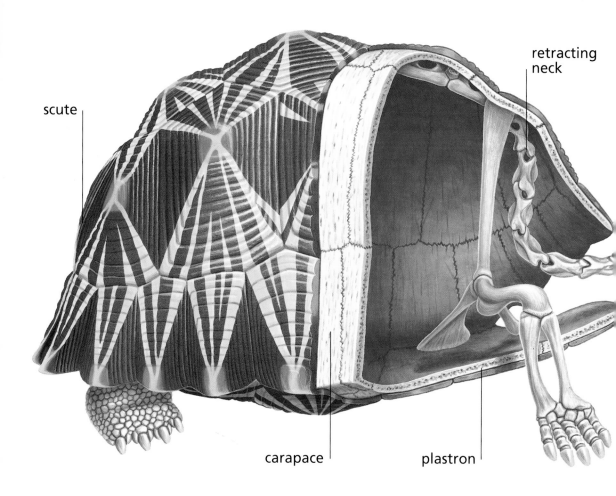

scute

retracting neck

carapace

plastron

SUITABLE SHELLS

A slow-moving land tortoise has a domed shell. A sea turtle has a streamlined shell for swimming.

pond turtle

sea turtle

semi-terrestrial turtle

INSIDE TORTOISES AND TURTLES

Tortoises and turtles are the only reptiles with bony shells connected to the rest of their skeleton. The upper shell is called the carapace. The bottom shell is called the plastron. A layer of large, horny plates, called scutes, covers the whole shell. Scutes are made of the same material as your fingernails. Underneath the scutes is another layer made of bony plates, which helps make the shell even stronger.

AMAZING!

The pancake tortoise has a flat, flexible shell. It squeezes into narrow crevices for protection. It wedges itself in by filling its lungs with air and pushing out its shell.

land tortoise

SALAMANDERS AND NEWTS

Salamanders and newts are amphibians. They look like lizards, but they don't have scales. Most salamanders start life as tiny larvae in water. They breathe through feathery gills and swim with flattened tails. As the larvae grow, they develop legs and climb out of the water. Some salamanders, however, lose their feathery gills as adults and live on land. All salamanders have to stay near water, to keep their slimy skins from drying out.

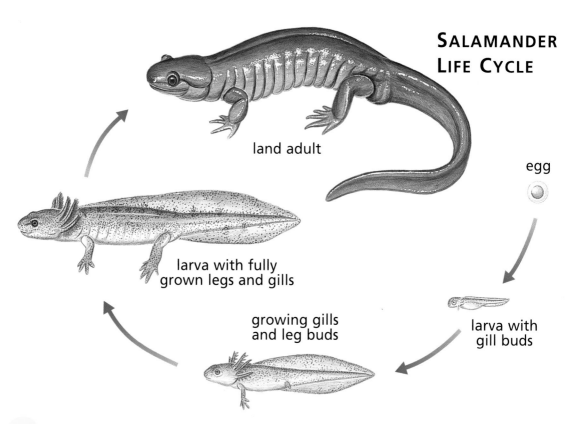

SALAMANDER LIFE CYCLE

land adult

egg

larva with fully grown legs and gills

growing gills and leg buds

larva with gill buds

NOISY GIANT

Most salamanders are silent. The Pacific giant salamander is unusual—it makes a low-pitched sound if it is disturbed.

DID YOU KNOW?

The mudpuppy salamander breathes through frilly red gills. People called it a mudpuppy because they thought it could bark—but it can't!

WATER NEWTS

Newts are a type of salamander. Most of them live in water.

FROGS AND TOADS

Frogs and toads are the most common amphibians. Most frogs start life as wiggly tadpoles swimming in ponds and streams, breathing through gills like a fish, and eating weeds. As a tadpole grows, it gets ready for life on land. It starts to use its lungs to breathe air. Its tail shrinks and it grows legs. Finally, it turns into a frog and leaves the water to eat insects. Soon it lays its own eggs, and the cycle starts again.

STRANGE BUT TRUE

The oriental fire-bellied toad flashes its brightly colored belly at predators, to warn them that its skin tastes terrible.

HANDLE WITH CARE

Some toads have enough poison in their skin glands to kill a dog that picks one up in its mouth!

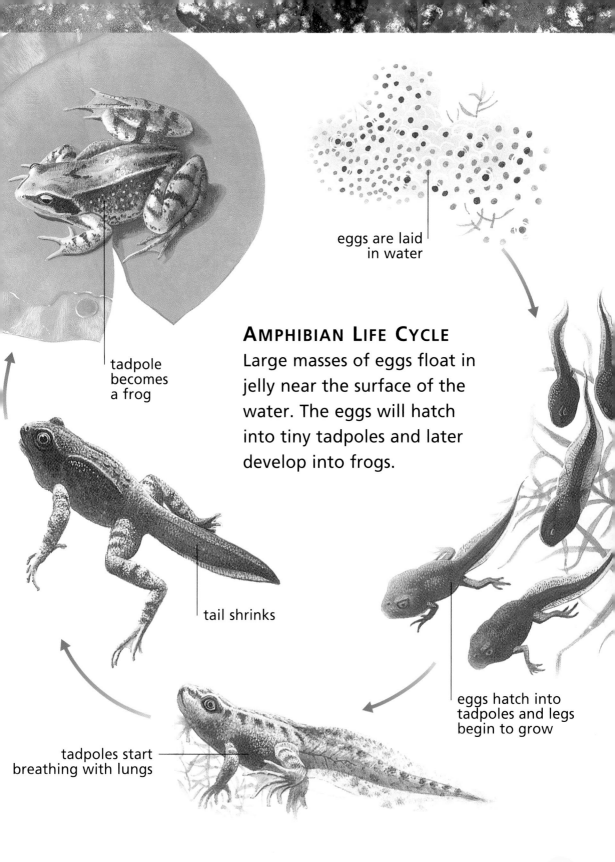

eggs are laid
in water

tadpole
becomes
a frog

AMPHIBIAN LIFE CYCLE
Large masses of eggs float in jelly near the surface of the water. The eggs will hatch into tiny tadpoles and later develop into frogs.

tail shrinks

eggs hatch into
tadpoles and legs
begin to grow

tadpoles start
breathing with lungs

flying gecko

wall lizard

LIZARD LIFE

There are about 3,750 types of lizards in the world. They can be found in almost every environment. The smallest lizard is a tiny gecko smaller than your finger. The biggest is the 10-foot (3-meter) long Komodo dragon. Legless lizards are long and thin and look like snakes. Some lizards are brightly colored, while others blend into the background. Most lizards are predators. They eat everything from ants and insects to other lizards.

short-horned lizard

monitor lizard

water dragon

legless lizard

PUFF LANGUAGE

The male anole lizard can puff out his dewlap (a flap of skin on his throat) to communicate with other anole lizards.

AMAZING!

This lizard lives in the desert. It uses its back legs and tail to "swim" through the sand.

STRANGE TAILS

Some lizards have a tail that drops off if it is grabbed by a predator. Others have a clublike tail that stores fat. Tails can also be used for camouflage, or for gripping when climbing.

Did You Know?

A tuatara hunts at night. It spends the day sleeping in its burrow or lying in the sunshine at the burrow entrance.

THE TUATARA

Tuataras have been around for much longer than any snakes or lizards that exist today. Some people call them living fossils. Even though they look like lizards, they are not. They belong to a group of reptiles that lived in the world when the dinosaurs were alive, 240 million years ago. By 60 million years ago they were extinct everywhere except New Zealand. Today, they can be found only on a few islands off the coast of New Zealand, where there are no rats to eat their eggs. Scientists think a tuatara can live as long as 120 years!

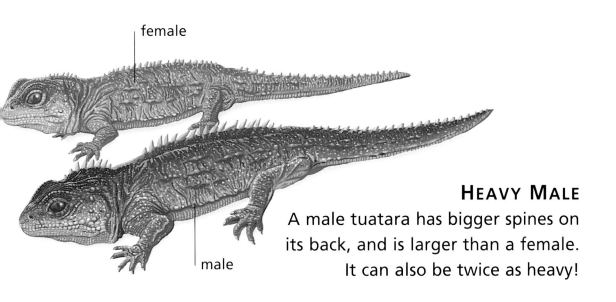

female

male

HEAVY MALE
A male tuatara has bigger spines on its back, and is larger than a female. It can also be twice as heavy!

python

horned viper

burrowing
snake

tree snake

DIFFERENT HEADS

A python has many teeth, so it has a large head. A viper has a short head and large fangs. A burrowing snake has a blunt head to push through soil. A tree snake has a slim head to help it slip between twigs.

SCALY SNAKES

Snakes have many different ways of killing their prey. Some snakes squeeze their prey to death, while others use venom, which comes out of long fangs. One type of venom works by stopping the heart. Another venom destroys the muscles so the animal cannot run. Snakes can swallow prey larger than themselves because they have elastic connections between the bones in their jaw. They eat everything from ants, eggs, and snails to small animals. The anaconda, which grows up to 36 feet (11 meters) long, squeezes its prey to death and can swallow a whole goat!

BRIGHT DANGER

The ringneck snake is sometimes called the corkscrew snake. When it is in danger, it twists itself into tight coils to show its bright belly.

BODY SHAPES

Snakes can be small and slim, short and thick-bodied, or large and shaped like a cylinder.

reticulated python

blind snake   viper

CROCODILIAN CHARACTERISTICS

Crocodiles and alligators are part of a group called the crocodilians, which also includes caimans and gavials. Crocodilians are the world's largest and most dangerous reptiles. They live in warm regions around the world, in and near the water. Their eyes and their nostrils are set high up on their head so they can hide under water, but can still see and breathe. They drift slowly toward their prey and then—pounce! Their teeth can only grip, not chew, so crocodilians swallow prey whole or shake the prey to break it into pieces.

kidney   stomach   lung

heart

INSIDE A CROCODILIAN
Stomach stones grind up large pieces of food so they can be digested.

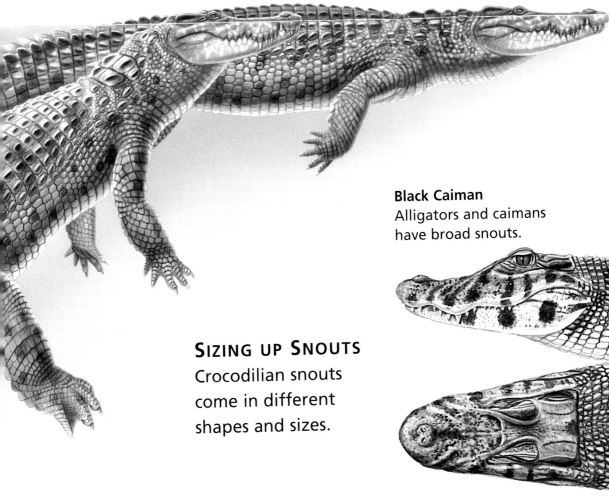

Black Caiman
Alligators and caimans have broad snouts.

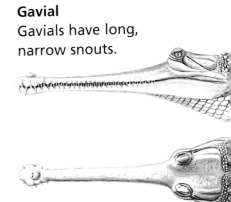

Sizing up Snouts
Crocodilian snouts come in different shapes and sizes.

Gavial
Gavials have long, narrow snouts.

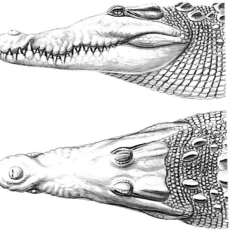

American Crocodile
When a crocodile closes its mouth, the fourth tooth in the bottom jaw sticks out.

Alligators and caimans are closely related. Unlike crocodiles, they both have bottom teeth that are hidden when their mouths are closed. Alligators have large, rounded teeth, while caimans have sharp, narrow teeth. Male gavials have a knob on their nose that makes a buzzing noise, warning other males to stay away. Crocodiles are dangerous hunters, often ambushing land animals when they come to drink. The crocodile grabs its prey, pulls it under water, and then twists and spins its body to tear the prey to pieces.

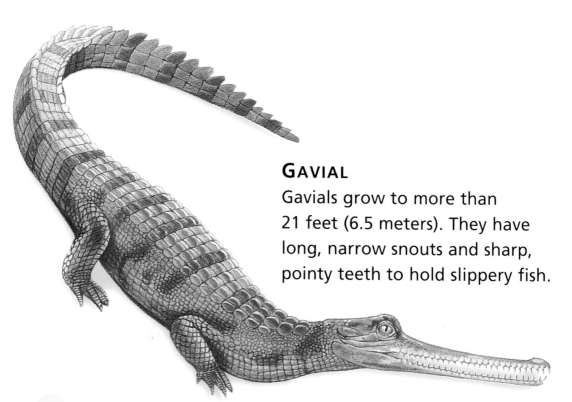

GAVIAL
Gavials grow to more than
21 feet (6.5 meters). They have
long, narrow snouts and sharp,
pointy teeth to hold slippery fish.

AMERICAN CROCODILE

American crocodiles can grow to more than 20 feet (6 meters). They eat fish, mammals, birds—and sometimes people.

AMERICAN ALLIGATOR

American alligators grow to about 20 feet (6 meters). They can leap right out of the water to catch prey.

DID YOU KNOW?

An alligator's jaws can be deadly, but mothers also use them to carry babies. Unlike most reptiles, female crocodilians look after their eggs and young until they are grown.

29

GLOSSARY

camouflage Something in an animal's appearance that allows it to blend into its surroundings, so it can stay safe, or catch food.

cold-blooded A description for an animal whose body temperature changes according to the temperature outside the animal's body.

desert An area that receives little or no moisture during the year.

environment The natural surroundings of a place.

evolved A description of a plant or animal whose body or habits have gradually changed in ways that allow it to live more successfully in its environment.

fangs Long, sharp teeth that spiders and snakes use to inject poison into their prey.

gills Organs that allow sea creatures, such as fish, to get oxygen from water instead of breathing it from the air.

predators Animals that hunt and kill other animals.

prey Animals that are caught and eaten by other animals.

reptiles Cold-blooded animals that have backbones and dry skin covered by scales or a hard shell.

scutes The horny plates on a crocodile's back or covering a turtle's shell.

venom Poison that is injected by certain animals to attack enemies, or by plants to trap food.

INDEX

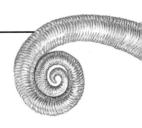

PICTURE AND ILLUSTRATION CREDITS

[t=top, b=bottom, l=left, r=right, c=center, F=front, B=back, C=cover, bg=background]

Anne Bowman 26bl. **Corel Corporation** 12c, 17tr, 17bl, 21tl, 25tr, 4–32 borders, Cbg. **Simone End** 7bc, 12tr, 20tc, 21b, 31r. **John Francis/Bernard Thornton Artists UK** 6–7c. **David Kirshner** 1c, 2b, 3tr, 4br, 10–11tc, 10bc, 14c, 14–15b, 16c, 17c, 18br, 18cl, 20l, 21c, 26–27c, 27c, 27r, 29br. **Frank Knight** 7tc, 9r, 19c. **James McKinnon** 22tl, 22br, 23bc, 30bc, FCc. **Colin Newman** 4–5rc, 8–9bl, 8tl, 13c. **Tony Pyrzakowski** 28–29tc, 28bl, 29c. **Trevor Ruth** 24tl, 25bl.

BOOKS IN THIS SERIES